Ming Shu

Your Personal Daily Horoscope

Ming Shu

Your Personal Daily Horoscope

For those born in the Year of the Dragon

Derek Walters

Lyndhurst Press
Bath, England

First published in 2021 by Lyndhurst Press
Norton St Philip
Bath
BA2 7LH
UK

ISBN: 978-1-914323-04-1

Contents

Introduction

Our Destiny! Are we the rulers of our Fate? Are our lives shaped merely by chance circumstances? Or is the future already mapped out for us?

Few people, whatever their beliefs, could honestly say that future events hold little interest for them. Every day, millions of people worldwide scan the astrology columns in their newspapers and magazines, while at fairs, festivals and seaside resorts, fortune tellers are sure to be a popular attraction.

But for many Chinese people, a consultation with the seer at a local temple is a cultural obligation not to be undertaken lightly. Particularly at the time of the Chinese New Year, but in fact on any day of the week, worshippers will visit Chinese temples, such as the Wong Tai Sin Temple in Hong Kong, or the ancient Lung Shan Temple in Taipei, in order to find out from the soothsayers there what the prospects are for their business success, health and future happiness.

From the beginning of recorded history, cultures throughout the world have observed that the seasonal changes on which agriculture depends are ruled by the Sun, while the rise and fall of the tides follow the Moon's phases. It is a remarkable coincidence that from Earth, the daytime Sun and the nocturnal Moon appear to be exactly the same size in the sky.

For the dedicated observer of the Heavens, the motions of the celestial bodies present many more mysterious correspondences. For example, the planet Jupiter takes as many years to travel through the heavens as there are phases of the Moon in an Earth year, while the planet Saturn takes as many years to traverse the sky as there are days in the Moon's phases. So is it not logical to deduce that events on earth can be linked to the stars, planets and other celestial manifestations?

In ancient China, it was considered that the courses of the planets and changes in the appearances of the stars were messages for the Emperor, the Emperor himself being represented by the pole star round which all the other stars rotate, or in the words of Confucius, 'make obeisance'.

Stars close to the pole star signified members of the Emperor's family, and the stars surrounding them were the ministers, generals and nobility. As these stars twinkled, glimmered, brightened or faded, so the fortunes of the court officials were revealed.

As the Chinese empire grew, its traders and merchants became more prosperous. Although they were not important enough to have their own stars in the sky, they were sufficiently well off to persuade the temple monks to cast horoscopes for them. Only the official court astrologers were allowed to study the motions of the stars and planets, but the soothsayers were adept enough to realise that progressions of the Sun and Moon were sufficiently regular and ordered to enable horoscopes to be cast based solely on the day and time of birth. Accordingly, a new branch of astrology developed in China, Ming Shu, meaning literally 'the Calculation of Fate'.

In the course of time, the temple astrologer began to play a role as important as a registrar of births, marriages and deaths, as these were the occasions when he was most likely to be in demand. It is still the case today, with the forecourts of many Chinese temples having side booths where authorised astrologers can be consulted. In Taiwan, old customs are carefully maintained as a way of life. At the principal temples there are so many astrologers at work that their booths overflow the temple grounds into the streets and the subways below, with some consultants linked to their clients by telephones and laptops. Even in mainland China, where 'superstitious practices' are often frowned upon, orange-robed priests and lay consultants sit patiently in the quiet temples, deftly applying brush-stroke calligraphy to the red paper horoscopes which are still eagerly sought by the faithful.

According to Chinese tradition, when a child is born, an astrologer is called on to cast his or her horoscope, and this is usually sealed and kept in a special box throughout the child's life. Often, too, marriages will not be contracted between two families until both parties have consulted their astrologers to ensure that the couple's horoscopes show that they are a compatible pair.

But as the Chinese New Year approaches, families from Hong Kong to San Francisco, even if they do not go to the expense of employing a professional astrologer to see what the coming year holds in store for them, are likely to buy the latest annual Tung Shu or 'everything book', the almanac with its store of household hints, first aid advice and predictions for every day of the year. This is hung up at home in a prominent place, where it can be consulted for daily directions and advice on almost every conceivable action, from digging trenches to washing hair. At first, a Western reader may find this odd, forgetting perhaps that in the Western world certain days are associated with particular activities, such as market day, early-closing day, even washday. There are even traditional days for eating certain foods: turkey at Christmas or Thanksgiving, fish on Fridays, Sunday roast dinner, or Pancake Tuesday. But for many Chinese readers, the observations in the almanac are not only for social convenience, they also assure happiness in the life to come.

By the time a thriving trade had opened up the vast continent of Asia, the Chinese system of astrology was firmly established according to theories that were quite different from those of the

Western world. For example, in western Asia many of the patterns of stars which shape the constellations have names such as Fish and Crab, reminiscent of the sea, whereas the constellation names used by Chinese astronomers are nearly always land-based, with references to buildings and markets. But in popular astrology the differences were even more remarkable.

For example, in popular Western astrology, a 'star sign' refers to the time of the year when someone was born. In China, however, a person's star sign refers to the actual year itself in which someone was born, so revealing a person's age!

The twelve animals of the Chinese zodiac are used both for twelve divisions of the day, and also for each year in a twelve-year cycle. Originally, Chinese astronomers used technical names for the different divisions. For example, the start of the day was originally indicated by a sign which signified a baby, and the same sign was used to mark the first year of the cycle of twelve years, suggesting the birth of a new time period. Likewise, the seventh sign, halfway through the sequence, was represented by a sign signifying a balance, in the same way that Libra, the Scales, stands at the halfway point of the Western zodiac.

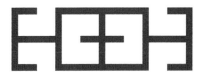

If there are enough foxes a fur coat can be made from the hair of their armpits.

Many insignificances can amount to a substantial total

A man on a mountain side would have to sit for a long time with his mouth open before a roast duck flew into it.

An admonition of hopeless optimism

The Twelve Animals of Chinese Astrology

Many centuries ago, the twelve signs became to be more popularly known by a list of animals. Exactly when or where the animal names actually originated is still disputed, but it was a brilliant idea which soon became the usual way of reckoning the hours and years across the whole of Asia, from Japan through China and Mongolia, and as far west as Turkey.

The animal names are usually translated as Rat, Ox, Tiger, Rabbit, Dragon, Snake, Horse, Sheep, Monkey, Rooster, Dog and Pig. There are often variations in translation, such as Mouse, Cow, Hare and Goat for Rat, Ox, Rabbit and Sheep, and so on, but usually there is no difference in actual significance. There is one exception to this rule: there is definitely no cat! Occasionally, writers replace the Rabbit/Hare with this intruder because in some south-eastern Chinese languages the word for hare is considered impolite.

It is worth noting that every sign is an animal, whereas the Western zodiac includes people: Gemini, the Twins; Virgo, a maiden or virgin; Sagittarius, the Archer; Aquarius, the Water-carrier; and even an object: a pair of scales! The Chinese signs are all creatures in a celestial 'zoo', literally a true 'zoo-diac'.

The Twielve Animals of Chinese Astrology in traditional papercut design

For years in the twentieth century it is relatively easy to calculate the animal sign for the year since all years for which the last two digits were divisible by 12 (e.g. 1972, 1984) are Rat years, and the animal signs for the required year can be found just by counting back or forward to the nearest Rat year. For years in the present century however, years for which the last two digits are divisible by 12 (e.g. 2012, 2024) are Dragon years, and the Rat years are four years earlier (2008, 2020).

YIN AND YANG

The twelve animal signs are grouped into six pairs. The first of each pair is considered to have '*yang*' or active attributes, while the second possesses softer '*yin*' qualities. Thus, the impetuous Rat is paired with the contemplative Ox; the fighting Tiger with the gentle Rabbit; the extrovert Dragon with the secretive Snake; the competitive Horse with the sociable Sheep; the ingenious Monkey with the shrewd Rooster; and the adventurous Dog with the home-loving Pig.

According to Chinese beliefs, all things are made from differing proportions of *yin* and *yang*. They can be likened to both sides of a coin, in that you cannot have one side without the other. More practically, they represent 'female / male', or 'passive / active', but without the connotations of bad or good, any more than the 'negative / positive' poles of batteries are bad or good. Thus in any one personality, *yin* and *yang* represent the opposing sides of human character, the imaginative and the logical, as well as the creative and the destructive. *Yang* is a quality, *yin* is its complement.

The reason we say '*yin and yang*' rather than '*yang and yin*' is purely a matter of speech tones; it is natural for the first of any pair of words to have a higher pitch than the word which follows.

THE SIX HOUSES OF THE CHINESE ZODIAC

Each *yang-yin* pair of animal signs combines to form one of the six aspects of destiny known to astrologers as 'Houses'. They reveal the likely trends of fortune for different periods of time, whether years, months, days, or hours.

The six pairs of animal signs comprise:

1 – the Rat and Ox, which together represent the beginnings and completions of projects in the *House of Construction*;

2 – the Tiger and Rabbit, symbolising the aggressive and diplomatic paths to personal achievement in the *House of Expansion*;

3 – the Dragon and Snake reflect the extrovert and introspective sides of personality in the *House of Mystery*;

4 – the Horse and Sheep reveal the differences in interests and attitudes shown by both sexes in the *House of Gender*;

5 – the Monkey and Rooster display craftsmanship and artistry in the *House of Career*;

6 – the Dog and Pig, symbolising home and its comforts, as well as offspring, in the *House of Family*.

PERSONALITY REVEALED

Many people, when they first encounter Chinese astrology, find it hard to accept the general principle that everyone born in a particular year will have the same basic personal characteristics. But in fact this is one of Chinese astrology's most convincing factors. Teachers in schools and colleges which have yearly intakes often observe that, taken as a whole, the students from one year will have general characteristics which distinguish them from the students of other years, just as wine merchants recognise that the qualities of one year's vintage differ from those of other years.

The principles of Chinese astrology also consider other time factors such as the animal sign of the hour when a person was born, as this is said to have an important bearing on future career and happiness. A more detailed picture of personality and fate can be assessed and modified by the animal types associated with the month or season of birth in the year of birth. For example, someone born in a Rat year would have the Rat characteristics emphasised if born in a Rat month, but lessened if born in the month of the Horse – the Rat's opposite sign. In detailed Chinese horoscopes, the Year, Season, Day and Time of birth are called the 'Four Pillars' of the horoscope, a distinctive feature which Marco Polo considered worthy of mention in his account of his travels through Asia.

COMPATIBILITY BETWEEN ANIMAL TYPES

Once you are familiar with your own animal sign, you will no doubt want to know the signs of others close to you, and then to establish the nature and extent of your compatibility. Compatible signs are the ones next but one in the series, Dog and Rat, Rat and Tiger, or Ox and Rabbit, for example.

INCOMPATIBLE ANIMAL SIGNS

Just as certain combinations are considered favourable, others are adverse. To assess these relationships, it helps to imagine the animals in a circle, like positions on a clock face. Those signs which stand opposite each other on the clock face, such as Rat and Horse, or Rabbit and Rooster, are particularly adverse to each other. Also inauspicious are clock face positions which are three hours apart such as Ox and Dragon (at hour positions 1 and 4), or Snake and Monkey (at hour positions 5 and 8).

Reverse pairs, such as Pig and Rat, are not compatible either, even though they are next to each other in the sequence of signs. They are like two pieces of broken china from different objects; they may look as though they should fit, but they do not belong to each other.

Fortunately, unfavourable combinations can always be remedied if a compensating animal sign is present in the horoscope, and if such a sign is missing, it can be compensated for by actively introducing something to represent it in daily life.

ELEMENTS COMPATIBILTY

In Chinese astrology, it is a well-established precept that two people will be compatible if their influencing elements stand next to each other in the generative order. So, a Wood-type person is supported by a Water-type, and supports a Fire-type. But remember that Fire is *supported* by Wood; Fire does not destroy it. The 'destructive' order is when alternate elements follow each other: Wood – Earth – Water – Fire – Metal. In the destructive order, Wood is said to absorb all the goodness from Earth; Earth pollutes Water; Water quenches Fire; Fire melts Metal; and Metal chops down Wood.

From these two orders, it is easy to see how one element type may either help or hinder another. Positively, a Wood-type may provide the Fire person with resources; the Fire-type may stimulate the obstinate Earth; Earth may give stability to the rash Metal-type; Metal may give active support to the dreaming Water personality; and Water may provide the knowledge from which the Wood-type is able to create.

Conversely, the Wood-type may be a drain on the Earth's resources, perhaps of patience or even materially; an Earth-type could cause damage to Water's reputation; Water may quench the Fire-type's enthusiasm; Fire would be a very formidable opponent for an abnormally assertive Metal-type, who in turn might harass Wood.

THE FIVE ELEMENTS AND MUSICAL NOTES

An unexpected quality of the Five Elements is their association with musical notes; Although this might seem to be a highly specialised topic it is far-reaching. In common with much traditional music throughout the world, Chinese music is pentatonic, its melodies and structure require only five different notes. Very conveniently these are matched by the black notes of a piano and it can be readily demonstrated that tunes such as 'Amazing Grace' and 'Auld Lang Syne' can be played using only the black keys of a piano, thus revealing that these melodies are themselves pentatonic. The fact that Chinese music is based on five notes is not an arbitrary classification but its inherent feature. That the five notes relate to the Five Elements is revealed in one of the earliest recorded inferences to the Five Elements, not directly to the element names, but to their astrological associations. Predictions for the coming year were drawn from the overall hum of the crowds in the marketplace at the New Year. For example, 'If the sound made by the crowds is the note 'Gong' then the harvest will be good; if it is the note 'Shang' wars will break out. If it is the note 'Yü' the weather will be wet.

The names of the five notes, their associated elements and correspondence to international notation are:

Gong - Earth (doh); *Shang* - Metal (ray); *Jeh* - Wood (me);
Ji - Fire (soh); *Yü* - Water (la).

Fa and te are not present in the pentatonic scale.

The meanings of the Chinese note names are immaterial; the relevant feature of the name is its vowel sound. There is a perceptible rise in pitch when the names of the five notes are spoken in sequence. (You are able to hear this by whispering the names of the five Chinese notes. If the rise in pitch is not clear, try whispering these names: Wolf, Dog, Cat, Pet, Bee.)

The practical application of this phenomenon can be for choosing auspicious names for children, pets, or businesses.

Musical sounds were used for regulating weights and measures throughout the Chinese Empire. Standard length was determined by a musical pipe which produced the note Gong. In practice this would be a length of 81 fen (Chinese inches). This number, being repeatedly divisible by 3 was used to determine the exact lengths for pitches of the notes of the pentatonic scale.

A curious link exists between the piano keyboard and the calendar. If the white note F on the piano keyboard is said to be January and the black note to its right F sharp, with the other keys following the months in sequence, then all the white keys will represent months with 31 days, while the black keys represent the shorter months. Where there is no black key between the white keys, as at E/F and B/C the months represented include the Winter and Summer solstices.

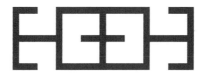

Charting Future Paths

But what of the future, whatever your animal type? Chinese astrologers maintain that the success or failure of plans can be foreseen not only by observing the assistance or conflicts which occur when two animal signs concur, but also by considering the elements associated with the progress of the project. Are the elements dominant, recessive, waxing or waning? By comparing the pattern of the animal signs and the associated elements of a particular day with those of the day when someone was born, Chinese astrologers are able to assess whether the day is likely to prove favourable or otherwise, and so advise appropriate courses of action specifically for that person.

The final section of this book shows you how to calculate a formula which compares the astrological aspects of a birth-date with those of a specific date in the near or distant future. Some people may claim that they do not wish to know what the future holds in store for them. But if there is danger ahead, is it not better to be forewarned? And if there is happiness in store, will it not give encouragement? Often, we are faced with crises and decisions. By perusing your daily horoscope aspect, and taking into consideration the prevailing fortunate elements, problems and dilemmas can often be untangled, and the right direction made clearer.

It is my sincere hope that the knowledge and advice gathered for you from the many friends I have met during my travels to the temples and monasteries throughout China and the Far East will bring you a deeper insight and understanding of your true self, and of your relationship with the world about you.

The Animal Signs for the Chinese Lunar Years

The Chinese lunar new year falls between mid-January and mid-February on a different date each year according to the phase of the Moon. The zodiac animal for any year begins with the date of the New Year and remains throughout the year until the start of the next Chinese New Year.

For people born between March and December, the relevant animal sign for their year can be read off from the table directly, but for someone born in January or February, it is important to check the precise date of the Chinese New Year. For example, someone born on March 1st 2002 would be a Water-Horse, but for a person born on February 11th, the day before the Chinese New Year, their zodiac sign is still the previous one, Metal-Snake.

The fact that the lunar new year tends to fall on the same date every nineteen years was observed by ancient astronomers.

YEAR	DATE	ANIMAL	YEAR	DATE	ANIMAL
1924	Feb 05	Wood-Rat	1938	Jan 31	Earth-Tiger
1925	Jan 25	Wood-Ox	1939	Feb 19	Earth-Rabbit
1926	Feb 13	Fire-Tiger	1940	Feb 08	Metal-Dragon
1927	Feb 02	Fire-Rabbit	1941	Jan 07	Metal-Snake
1928	Jan 23	Earth-Dragon	1942	Feb 15	Water-Horse
1929	Feb 10	Earth-Snake	1943	Feb 05	Water-Sheep
1930	Jan 30	Metal-Horse	1944	Jan 25	Wood-Monkey
1931	Feb 17	Metal-Sheep	1945	Feb 13	Wood-Rooster
1932	Feb 06	Water-Monkey	1946	Feb 02	Fire-Dog
1933	Jan 26	Water-Rooster	1947	Jan 22	Fire-Pig
1934	Feb 14	Wood-Dog	1948	Feb 10	Earth-Rat
1935	Feb 04	Wood-Pig	1949	Jan 29	Earth-Ox
1936	Jan 24	Fire-Rat	1950	Feb 17	Metal-Tiger
1937	Feb 11	Fire-Ox	1951	Feb 06	Metal-Rabbit

YEAR	DATE	ANIMAL	YEAR	DATE	ANIMAL
1952	Jan 27	Water-Dragon	1966	Jan 21	Fire-Horse
1953	Feb 14	Water-Snake	1967	Feb 09	Fire-Sheep
1954	Feb 03	Wood-Horse	1968	Jan 30	Earth-Monkey
1955	Jan 24	Wood-Sheep	1969	Feb 17	Earth-Rooster
1956	Feb 12	Fire-Monkey	1970	Feb 06	Metal-Dog
1957	Jan 31	Fire-Rooster	1971	Jan 27	Metal-Pig
1958	Feb 18	Earth-Dog	1972	Feb 15	Water-Rat
1959	Feb 08	Earth-Pig	1973	Feb 05	Water-Ox
1960	Jan 28	Metal-Rat	1974	Jan 23	Wood-Tiger
1961	Feb 15	Metal-Ox	1975	Feb 11	Wood-Rabbit
1962	Feb 05	Water-Tiger	1976	Jan 31	Fire-Dragon
1963	Jan 25	Water-Rabbit	1977	Feb 18	Fire-Snake
1964	Feb 13	Wood-Dragon	1978	Feb 07	Earth-Horse
1965	Feb 02	Wood-Snake	1979	Jan 28	Earth-Sheep

YEAR	DATE	ANIMAL	YEAR	DATE	ANIMAL
1980	Feb 16	Metal-Monkey	1994	Feb 10	Wood-Dog
1981	Feb 05	Metal-Rooster	1995	Jan 31	Wood-Pig
1982	Jan 25	Water-Dog	1996	Feb 19	Fire-Rat
1983	Feb 13	Water-Pig	1997	Feb 07	Fire-Ox
1984	Feb 02	Wood-Rat	1998	Jan 28	Earth-Tiger
1985	Feb 20	Wood-Ox	1999	Feb 16	Earth-Rabbit
1986	Feb 09	Fire-Tiger	2000	Feb 05	Metal-Dragon
1987	Jan 29	Fire-Rabbit	2001	Jan 24	Metal-Snake
1988	Feb 17	Earth-Dragon	2002	Feb 12	Water-Horse
1989	Feb 06	Earth-Snake	2003	Feb 01	Water-Sheep
1990	Jan 27	Metal-Horse	2004	Jan 22	Wood-Monkey
1991	Feb 15	Metal-Sheep	2005	Feb 09	Wood-Rooster
1992	Feb 04	Water-Monkey	2006	Jan 29	Fire-Dog
1993	Jan 23	Water-Rooster	2007	Feb 18	Fire-Pig

YEAR	DATE	ANIMAL	YEAR	DATE	ANIMAL
2008	Feb 07	Earth-Rat	2021	Feb 12	Metal-Ox
2009	Jan 26	Earth-Ox	2022	Feb 01	Water-Tiger
2010	Feb 14	Metal-Tiger	2023	Jan 22	Water-Rabbit
2011	Feb 03	Metal-Rabbit	2024	Feb 10	Wood-Dragon
2012	Jan 23	Water-Dragon	2025	Jan 29	Wood-Snake
2013	Feb 10	Water-Snake	2026	Feb 17	Fire-Horse
2014	Jan 31	Wood-Horse	2027	Feb 06	Fire-Sheep
2015	Feb 19	Wood-Sheep	2028	Jan 26	Earth-Monkey
2016	Feb 08	Fire-Monkey	2029	Feb 13	Earth-Rooster
2017	Jan 28	Fire-Rooster	2030	Feb 02	Metal-Dog
2018	Feb 16	Earth-Dog	2031	Jan 23	Metal-Pig
2019	Feb 05	Earth-Pig			
2020	Jan 25	Metal-Rat			

When farmers stack hay the last of the crop goes on the top.

The last resort is not the best solution

A picture of a snake is not improved by drawing legs on it

Superfluous activity ruins the original plan

The Dragon Personality

The Dragon personality is a lover of the exotic, and is one of the most flamboyant and extrovert characters of the Chinese astrological calendar. Elegant and with a good eye for fashion, Dragon types are always ready to adapt the latest trend to suit their own individual whims.

With an extraordinarily fertile imagination, the Dragon is forever dreaming up fresh schemes and ideas for new ventures, few of which are wholly practical. Such a mercurial character can be the despair of friends, and at work can lead to chaos. The Dragon has to be surrounded by practical people to pick up the fragments of abandoned projects, and they frequently resent it. Strong, decisive and resolute in their determination to follow interesting tracks which may lead nowhere, Dragons would become wealthy were it not for the fact that spectacular gains are as often as not offset by the money wasted on trivial things.

The sign of the Dragon is also an indication of an interest in the mysterious, the supernatural and the occult. Dragon types are surrounded by an aura of good fortune. It is said, however, that this disperses immediately a Rabbit personality appears on the scene.

PEOPLE BORN AND NOTABLE EVENTS
IN THE YEAR OF THE DRAGON

Salvador Dali, Ringo Starr, Boris Johnson,
Kamala Harris, and Adele.

1928 Dr. Alexander Fleming discovered Penicillin while working in St. Mary's Hospital London.

2012 Austrian skydiver, Felix Baumgartner, breaks the world record by jumping from more than 24 miles above Earth, breaking the speed of sound during his descent.

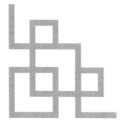

HOW THE FIVE ELEMENTS
AFFECT THE DRAGON PERSONALITY

The Wood-Dragon
13 Feb 1964 – 1 Feb 1965; 10 Feb 2024 – 28 Jan 2025

The Wood-Dragon is a creative artist, the painter of pictures on a grand scale: bold, daring and colourful. A creator of style and fashion, not its follower, this personality is not bound by convention, and is happiest when setting projects into motion. The Wood-Dragon is full of great ideas, but cares little for detail or practicality. In romantic matters, this type may have tremendous sex appeal, but it is often vexing for a long-suffering partner. In marriage, the Wood-Dragon is likely to fare best with someone born in a Water year.

The Fire-Dragon
31 Jan 1976 – 17 Feb 1977

The Fire element heightens the Dragon's love of the exotic, and both intelligence and a lively mind may lead this type to investigate the obscure and mysterious. This is especially so if there is a chance that it can bring personal recognition. Great spenders, Fire-Dragons are rarely afraid of going into debt. In love, they can be passionate and adventurous. Partners born in Wood and Earth years form the most stable relationship.

The Earth-Dragon
23 Jan 1928 – 9 Feb 1929; 17 Feb 1988 – 5 Feb 1989
The Earth element has a sound, stabilising effect on the Dragon personality. The more extravagant aspects are less in evidence, and varied interests, no matter how seemingly eccentric, will always have a practical purpose. In romance, Earth-Dragons make imaginative lovers, and form more lasting attachments than other Dragon types. They get on well with most element types, save those born in Water years.

The Metal-Dragon
8 Feb 1940 – 26 Jan 1941; 5 Feb 2000 – 23 Jan 2001
The Dragon born in a Metal year encounters many changes of fortune. There is rarely a shortage of ready money, but financial security seems to be forever elusive. Such people tend to tread on knife edges, taking risks and living dangerously. Most succeed, but some fall by the wayside. Metal-Dragons also tend to be extremely jealous lovers. In the long term, they fare best with partners born in Water years.

The Water-Dragon
27 Jan 1952 – 13 Feb 1953; 23 Jan 2012 – 9 Feb 2013
A love of the mystical and occult is indicated by the Water element. Water-Dragons will be fascinated by strange rites, cults and secret societies. Avid readers themselves, they may be inclined to try their hand at writing science fiction. In love, they like to weave an aura of mystery round their romances. Water-Dragons should try to find someone born in a Metal year for their best partner in marriage.

HOW THE HOUR OF BIRTH
AFFECTS THE DRAGON PERSONALITY

Born during the Rat hour (11 pm – 1 am)
The Midnight Hour

Life will be happy, and will bring its rewards in many ways, if not financially. Special skills and abilities are indicated. Take care of health, be wise in the choice of life's companion, and do not strive for fame or honours.

Born during the Ox hour (1 am – 3 am)

Fortune comes from estate and land, but it also brings its problems. You are gifted with intelligence, but must avoid bring over-ambitious, lest everything is lost in speculation.

Born during the Tiger hour (3 am – 5 am)

The signs are excellent for the adventurous and those who wish to travel or settle abroad; an exotic career is promised, while a settled and stable home life is unlikely. Romances are quickly over, but a secure marriage is a possibility.

Born during the Rabbit hour (5 am – 7 am)
The Dawn Hour

There may be a difficult life ahead, with indecision and discontent marring the road to happiness. More than one marriage is foreseen, while ill-health may be a cause of anxiety if you take insufficient care. There are good prospects for travel and for intellectual achievement.

Born during the Dragon hour (7 am – 9 am)

The positive aspects of the basic personality – elegance, business sense and intuition – are highlighted. You have tremendous flair, and a love of the bizarre or supernatural. There may be many lucky chances in life, but carelessness could lose you a fortune.

Born during the Snake hour (9 am – 11 am)

You have a great love of the mysterious and exotic, and are something of a philosopher. Fame and fortune are possible, especially in a career connected with the legal profession. Travel and manufacture are less favourable. Family and children need particular care.

Born during the Horse hour (11 am – 1 pm)
The Noonday Hour

You are likely to make an impact when young, but should avoid becoming stale. The well of inventiveness may dry up, so it is important to decide future prospects early in life, especially as with age may come ill-health. Romance may bring its heartaches.

Born during the Sheep hour (1 pm – 3 pm)

Romance seems to be full of disappointments, so be careful not to waste time or money on unreliable partners. Later life is more secure, when children will bring happiness. Health is good.

Born during the Monkey hour (3 pm – 5 pm)

Birth at this hour brings favourable prospects for the potential to excel in manual skills and crafts. There is less emphasis on family life and matters dealing with children – such things have to take their own course. Avoid confrontations, bad company and risk-taking.

Born during the Rooster hour (5 pm – 7 pm)
The Sunset Hour

The signs are excellent if you seek your fortune on the stage, though less favourable if you look for happiness through romance, or a family with many children. On the road to a successful career, a healthy regime must be followed.

Born during the Dog hour (7 pm – 9 pm)

Avoid any suspect dealings regarding property speculation. Fortune will smile occasionally, but take great care that unexpected windfalls are not treated as a regular source of income. A happy marriage is foreseen, with a busy life involving much travelling.

Born during the Pig hour (9 pm – 11 pm)

Domestic harmony will have its more difficult moments, mainly due to the attractions of numerous interests beyond the home confines. Children may be unsettled; a sound educational upbringing needs to be considered. Health is good, and life is long.

HOW THE DRAGON PERSONALITY FARES IN EACH ANIMAL YEAR

In the Year of the Rat

This is an excellent year for the Dragon native. It is an ideal time to open up a new line of activity. Business, romance and health are at their best. Take advantage of all the opportunities the year offers.

In the Year of the Ox

Ancient astrological principles do not hold this year to be a good one for the Dragon personality. For the artistic or creative Dragon, it will be a discouraging period, and a particularly bad one for the gambler and risk-taker, too. But routine work will bring rewards. On the positive side, travel is favourable. Romance plays a significant role, but there is also a hint of scandal.

In the Year of the Tiger

The Dragon and the Tiger are astrologically harmonious, which indicates a fortunate year with opportunities for advancement in business and romantic affairs. The year also promises dangerous alliances, however. Dragon types will realise their ambitions, but, too late, will find that the strings round the more attractive packages are very firmly tied.

In the Year of the Rabbit

This is a moderate year for the Dragon. A fallow year, it is, however, a vital period of recuperation, even though to the Dragon it will seem routine and dull. The Dragon will have to be content with a time of stability, and dine out on last year's stories.

In the Year of the Dragon

For the Dragon personality, this is a year of spectacular achievement and personal success. The romantically inclined Dragon will have several opportunities to practise dalliance, while those who are more serious in their intentions may find that their ideal partner has at last entered the scene.

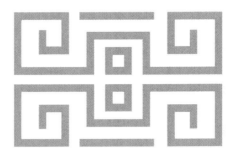

In the Year of the Snake

This year, many of the Dragon's more elaborate schemes and plans bear fruit, including those that were the object of derision when first mooted. The proof of considerable investments lies in their returns, which will vindicate the Dragon's faith in all such projects.

In the Year of the Horse

Another bustling year for the effervescent Dragon. Life is very active socially, and considerable pleasure can be expected from the numerous contacts made. As usual, money will be spent profusely – but this year, rather more rationally. There is the possibility of the Dragon forming a lasting, but stormy, relationship with someone from a completely different social set.

In the Year of the Sheep
The usually exuberant personality of the Dragon may for once be stifled by hurtful criticism. Fortunes are generally at an ebb. The Dragon should curb spending and speculation, as gambling losses feature very prominently in the chart.

In the Year of the Monkey
Dragon types exceed themselves this year. Having established a well-deserved reputation for eccentricity, they now put their more extraordinary schemes into practice. Some of these wild ideas will pay dividends. However, it is a pity that the Dragon tends to be accordingly lavish, and very little is left at the end of the year.

In the Year of the Rooster
The best aspects for the Dragon this year are those which concern the home, suggesting relocation. An unexpected financial gain could be followed by long-distance travel, and new proposals will find favour with those in authority. In business and commerce, there are several peaks and troughs, and personal life does not run smoothly either.

In the Year of the Dog

The Dragon, which is the sign of luck, falls under the influence of the Dog this year, and it is thus a dangerous time for speculation. Attention should be paid to the home, since there may be adverse conditions there. Despite this, social and business life do well.

In the Year of the Pig

Fortunes gently rise and fall this year. There is plenty of opportunity for social activity, but unfortunately there may be conflicts and petty jealousies. This tends to mar romantic ambitions, and heartache is likely. Decisions may need be taken concerning improvements to the house, but construction is unfavourable in the present chart.

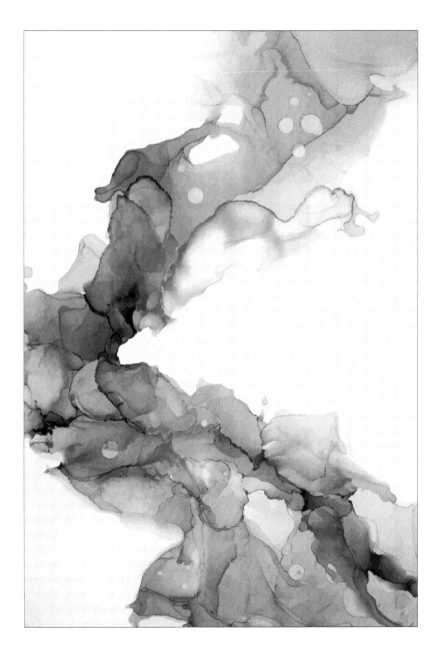

Relationships

Discover how each of the twelve animal signs relate to the Dragon, whether with reference to social relationships, friendships, interaction within the family, in business partnerships or long-term romance. The tables on pages 34-37 reveal which of the twelve animals rules a specific year.

With the Rat
Relations between Rat and Dragon types are very harmonious, leading to successful marriages and prosperous business partnerships. The artistic Rat child is likely to fulfil the Dragon parent's own latent ambitions.

With the Ox
The Ox and Dragon need to work hard together for an emotional relationship to last. In business, the Ox partner may be discontented. The Ox child is unlikely to share the parental Dragon's interests.

With the Tiger
This should be a very stable relationship for two individuals who recognise each other's talents. In business, the Tiger and Dragon make a high-flying team. But unless the Dragon parent recognises the Tiger child's individuality, conflicts may arise out of concern for the offspring's safety and well-being.

With the Rabbit
This is not the best of partnerships, as mutual understanding does not come easily. In business, particularly, confidence is lacking. Dragon parents will find that Rabbit children are determined to go their own ways.

With another Dragon
Most remarkable is the dynamic business association and unpredictable personal relationship two Dragons inevitably make. The Dragon child will certainly enjoy the Dragon parent's lively company.

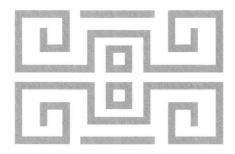

With the Snake
The Snake's cunning and the Dragon's flair are ideally suited to partnership, both in business and romance. The parental Dragon will be pleased with the Snake child's commonsense and logic.

With the Horse
A very sensible choice: the flamboyant Dragon needs to keep in touch with reality, and whether in business or love, the Horse proves a reliable partner. The Horse child will be better organised than the Dragon parent is perhaps ready to admit.

With the Sheep
This relationship is usually founded on infatuation, with a long-lasting partnership in either business or romance only being achieved with difficulties. The sensitive Sheep child needs great understanding and attention on the part of the parental Dragon.

With the Monkey

A Monkey and a Dragon may seem to make an alarming partnership, but in matters of love there is a deep understanding between them. They also make a remarkable business team. The gifted Monkey child will be a good companion for the parental Dragon.

With the Rooster

There is too much self-concern on both sides for this to be an ideal personal relationship. Business partnerships are marred by differences of opinion. The Dragon parent often finds the Rooster child assertively independent.

With the Dog

The Dog and Dragon are so opposite in nature that they actually complement each other. The Dog child, however, may be secretly contemptuous of the Dragon parent, and it will be important not to lose the child's respect.

With the Pig

The Pig will always bear the burden of the Dragon's waywardness, but should not be expected to be happy doing so. In business, the Dragon may find the Pig unfocused. The Pig child may feel it is not getting the attention it deserves from a Dragon parent.

Never tie your shoes in a melon field nor adjust your hat beneath a plum tree.

Always make sure your activities are not open to misinterpretation

If an orchestra is a player short, don't add someone who can't play the zither.

Using faulty substitutes ruins the effectiveness of the whole.

How to Calculate Your Personal Daily Horoscope

Chinese astrology is able to offer much more practical information than merely revealing the complexities of someone's personality. It can provide specific advice and suggest solutions to a range of problems. For example, it can help you choose days that are most likely to offer the best prospects for business or a successful social event, and, conversely, it can warn when it may be rash to embark on a journey or plan a speculative venture.

The following pages set out the basic method for casting your own personal daily horoscope. No special skill is required, just an ability to add or subtract a few simple whole numbers. The resulting factors will be an exact match for those recorded in the Imperial Chinese calendar, the oldest in the world, and still in publication after more than 3,000 years.

THE STEMS AND BRANCHES,
OR DAILY NUMBER

From the distant past until the present time, the international calendar has not only divided time into years and months, but also into weeks of seven days. Weeks have continued their regular seven-day sequence without interruption quite independently of the changing years and months.

Along similar lines, the Chinese calendar identifies individual days by a system called the *Stems and Branches*, but whereas a week consists of only seven days, the sequence of *Stems and Branches* follows an unchanging cycle of sixty days which are independent of the year, season or month.

The ten stems and twelve branches run alongside so that *Yang* (odd numbered) stems are always paired with *yang branches* and *yin stems* (even numbers) with *yin branches*, making sixty 'pairs'.

They are China's oldest method of recording the dates of notable events.

Although 22 different Chinese characters are needed to write the ten *stems* and twelve *branches*, because the pairs follow in regular succession each pair can be conveniently numbered from 1 to 60 to give the *Daily Number*.

When Chinese astrologers set up a horoscope for a person they always record the *Stem-Branch* of the day of birth. This can then be compared to the *Stem-Branch* of any future date to reveal whether that day would be favourable for particular activities such as travel, marriage, business or other ventures.

As the *Stem-Branch* can be conveniently represented by the equivalent *Daily Number*, the following pages reveal how to calculate it for any birthdate, and compare it with any other date to assess whether the two dates are mutually beneficial. The *Stem and Branch* for the *Daily Number* is given in the table on page 65.

TO FIND THE DAILY NUMBER
FOR ANY GIVEN DATE

Because the *Stems and Branches* are independent of the Chinese lunar and solar calendars, the *Daily Number* for any date can be directly calculated from the standard international calendar and the tables in the following pages.

Only three factors are needed:

first, the *Daily Number* for January 1st of the year in question;

second, the number of days from January 1st to the specified date;

third, whether the chosen year is a leap year.

Step 1

From **Table A** (pages 70-72) jot down the year code for the required date.

(This is actually the Daily Number for December 31st of the previous year.)

Step 2

From **Table B** (page 73) note the month code for the required date.

(The month code relates to the number of days which have elapsed between January 1st and the start of the selected month.)

Step 3

Add the **calendar date** of the month to the **year code** and the **month code**.

Step 4

Only if the chosen year is a
leap year, and then only if the chosen
date is March 1st or later in the year,
add an extra 1 to the total of Step 3.

*(A leap year is one in which the last two digits of the year
are divisible by 4, for example 2024. Adding 1 for leap
years allows for the extra day in February.)*

Step 5

Reduce the total to 60 or less.

*(If the total at Step 4 is greater than 60, subtract 60; if
the total it is still greater than 60, continue subtracting 60
from the total until the resulting figure is 60 or less.)*

This final figure is the **Daily Number** for the **chosen
date.** If this is your own **Personal Daily Number [P]**
you should make a note of it for future use.

Because the Daily Number is irrespective of the
Chinese solar and lunar calendars, it can be calculated
for any birthdate, whatever the person's zodiac sign,
but the horoscope aspects which follow
are specific for the Dragon.

Daily Number	Stem-and-Branch		Daily Number	Stem-and-Branch	
1	wood	rat	31	wood	horse
2	wood	ox	32	wood	sheep
3	fire	tiger	33	fire	monkey
4	fire	hare	34	fire	rooster
5	earth	dragon	35	earth	dog
6	earth	snake	36	earth	pig
7	metal	horse	37	metal	rat
8	metal	sheep	38	metal	ox
9	water	monkey	39	water	tiger
10	water	rooster	40	water	hare
11	wood	dog	41	wood	dragon
12	wood	pig	42	wood	snake
13	fire	rat	43	fire	horse
14	fire	ox	44	fire	sheep
15	earth	tiger	45	earth	monkey
16	earth	hare	46	earth	rooster
17	metal	dragon	47	metal	dog
18	metal	snake	48	metal	pig
19	water	horse	49	water	rat
20	water	sheep	50	water	ox
21	wood	monkey	51	wood	tiger
22	wood	rooster	52	wood	hare
23	fire	dog	53	fire	dragon
24	fire	pig	54	fire	snake
25	earth	rat	55	earth	horse
26	earth	ox	56	earth	sheep
27	metal	tiger	57	metal	monkey
28	metal	hare	58	metal	rooster
29	water	dragon	59	water	dog
30	water	snake	60	water	pig

HOW TO CALCULATE DAILY HOROSCOPE ASPECTS FOR THE DRAGON

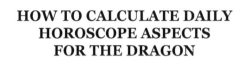

The *daily horoscope aspects* are found by comparing the **Daily Number of a Person** [P] with the **Daily Number of the Required Date** [D].

The method starts by following the same procedure outlined above, in **Steps 1 to 5**.

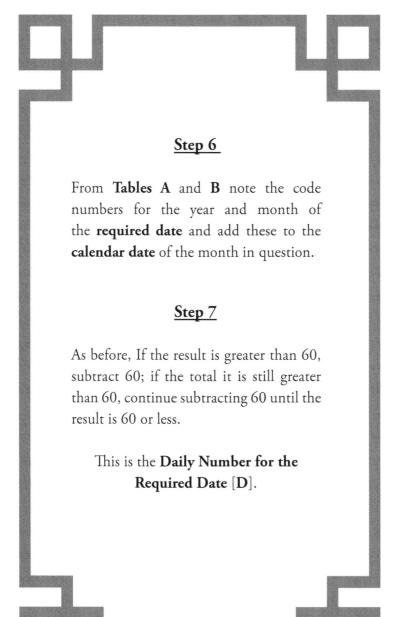

Step 6

From **Tables A** and **B** note the code numbers for the year and month of the **required date** and add these to the **calendar date** of the month in question.

Step 7

As before, If the result is greater than 60, subtract 60; if the total it is still greater than 60, continue subtracting 60 until the result is 60 or less.

This is the **Daily Number for the Required Date [D]**.

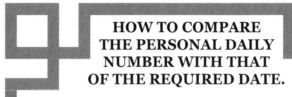

HOW TO COMPARE THE PERSONAL DAILY NUMBER WITH THAT OF THE REQUIRED DATE.

The next steps depend on whether the Personal Daily Number [P] is yang (odd) or yin (even).

Step 8a

If the **Personal Daily Number** [P] is odd, subtract it from the **Daily Number for the Required Date** [D].

(If the Daily Number for the Required Date is less than the Personal Daily Number, first add 60 to the Daily Number for the Required Date)

Step 8b

If the **Personal Daily Number** [P] is even, subtract the **Daily Number for the Required Date** [D] from the **Personal Daily Number**.

(If the Personal Daily Number is less than the Daily Number for the Required Date, first add 60 to the Personal Daily Number.)

<u>Step 9</u>

The result obtained at *Step 8* is your
Personal Daily Aspect [A]
for the date in question.

In mathematical terms:

if [P] is odd, then [A] = [D] - [P]

(if D is less than P, first add 60 to D)

if [P] is even, then [A] = [P] - [D]

(if P is less than D, first add 60 to P)

Pages 75-86 reveal what your Daily Aspect foretells.

In the event that the aspect for the chosen day is unfavourable, it is a simple matter to take a look at the aspects for the Daily Numbers close to the date originally chosen. Should one of the neighbouring aspects appear to be more promising, count the days between that date and the one originally selected, and consider the options.

TABLE A — YEAR CODES

YEAR	NUMBER	YEAR	NUMBER
1901	15	1928	36
1902	20	1929	42
1903	25	1930	47
1904	30	1931	52
1905	36	1932	57
1906	41	1933	3
1907	46	1934	8
1908	51	1935	13
1909	52	1936	18
1910	57	1937	24
1911	7	1938	29
1912	12	1939	34
1913	18	1940	39
1914	23	1941	45
1915	28	1942	50
1916	33	1943	55
1917	39	1944	0
1918	44	1945	6
1919	49	1946	11
1920	54	1947	16
1921	0	1948	21
1922	5	1949	27
1923	10	1950	32
1924	15	1951	37
1925	21	1952	42
1926	26	1953	48
1927	31	1954	53

TABLE A — YEAR CODES
(CONTINUED)

YEAR	NUMBER	YEAR	NUMBER
1955	58	1982	20
1956	3	1983	25
1957	9	1984	30
1958	14	1985	36
1959	19	1986	41
1960	24	1987	46
1961	30	1988	51
1962	35	1989	57
1963	40	1990	2
1964	45	1991	7
1965	51	1992	12
1966	56	1993	18
1967	1	1994	23
1968	6	1995	28
1969	12	1996	33
1970	17	1997	39
1971	22	1998	44
1972	27	1999	49
1973	33	2000	54
1974	38	2001	0
1975	43	2002	5
1976	48	2003	10
1977	54	2004	15
1978	59	2005	21
1979	4	2006	26
1980	9	2007	31
1981	15	2008	36

TABLE A — YEAR CODES
(CONTINUED)

YEAR	NUMBER	YEAR	NUMBER
2009	42	2025	6
2010	47	2026	11
2011	52	2027	16
2012	57	2028	21
2013	3	2029	27
2014	8	2030	32
2015	13	2031	37
2016	18	2032	42
2017	24	2033	48
2018	29	2034	53
2019	34	2035	58
2020	39	2036	3
2021	45	2037	9
2022	50	2038	14
2023	55	2039	19
2024	0	2040	24

TABLE B — MONTH CODES

MONTH	CODE NUMBER
January	0
February	31
March	59
April	30
May	0
June	31
July	1
August	32
September	3
October	35
November	4
December	34

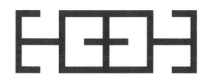

Prosperity

Luck

Longevity

Double Happiness

Daily Personal Horoscope Aspects for the Dragon

[**0**] See aspect 60.

[**I**] There will be a sudden stroke of luck today heralding highly favourable prospects and financial success, as well as exciting leisure activities in the evening.

[**2**] This will be a good day for dealing with people rather than things, since practical activities run into snags. There are, however, encouraging signs regarding the welfare of children. Plan rather than act today.

[**3**] This is a favourable day for all kinds of activity, so be prepared to find yourself doing more than you had planned as you juggle one task with another. Your expenditure will be greater than planned.

[**4**] Try to take things easily today. Rash actions may lead to accidents, and you may not be able to cope adequately with the heavy demands made upon you.

[**5**] This is a good day for making plans, and for anything involving construction, artistic activities or travel. Plan your time to get things done, and leave socialising, romance and leisure pursuits until another time.

[6] There are no significant signs for change, as matters progress as expected. Have confidence in following the usual procedures, both in business and in personal relationships.

[7] Be sure to use the favourable circumstances surrounding you today to their best advantage. There are better prospects for you elsewhere today, but do not go far.

[8] This is an uncomfortable day for dealings with colleagues or family in circumstances where you have to assert yourself. But, by keeping out of the spotlight, you will be able to learn profitably from other people's mistakes.

[9] A busy day ahead, with extra demands made on your time. Push ahead because in the end the results will be well worth it. You will know the outcome of a special matter shortly before sunset.

[10] Renewed strength and confidence will help you to obtain your objectives today, and there will be recognition and admiration for your recent diplomatic endeavours.

[11] Conditions remain generally unchanged, and all the minor irritations are still with you. You will just have to tolerate people's awkwardness a little longer. Stick to the tried and the trusted.

[12] This should be an ideal day for leisure activities, and romance is a possibility. While business ticks over, avoid dipping into your reserves. There is significant news from the south-east.

[13] You could find yourself involved in a lot of strenuous leisure activity today, for the accent appears to be on enjoyment. Avoid being carried away on a wave of euphoria.

[14] Things may seem to get on top of you today. Try not to get involved in open-ended situations. Plan ahead carefully, and keep objectives short-term. Be careful not to overspend.

[15] This is a good day for recreation, social activities, dealing with colleagues and friends, and for any romantic plans you may have. Arrange an excursion for the afternoon.

[**16**] The signs are generally harmonious and peaceful. At the end of the day, you may not have achieved as much as you would have liked, but there is plenty of time left.

[**17**] Conditions are very favourable today in all respects, but the prospects for home and family matters are highlighted. In formal matters, be guided by precedent.

[**18**] There are very good prospects for the Dragon today, and renewed vigour and self-confidence will enable you to succeed both in business and in personal matters.

[**19**] You will experience a very busy but highly successful day. Try to snatch a few moments to yourself, as you will need time to consider the implications of important news.

[**20**] Conditions are better for quiet creative planning, rather than trying to accomplish things before all the groundwork has been firmly established. Avoid gambling, or anything involving financial risk today.

[**21**] Use the present stable conditions to their best advantage. This is a good time for checking the progress of long-standing arrangements which need revising.

[**22**] The Dragon will find this an ideal day for purchases and commercial transactions generally. Business goes well, and personal relationships flourish.

[**23**] Do not worry that the day's progress has not yet brought the results you wanted. There are still plenty of opportunities for you to achieve your ambitions.

[**24**] The auspices for success are not favourable today. Rather than having to deal with unexpected problems, leave any decisions until you feel more confident. Avoid being drawn into pointless arguments.

[**25**] This is an ideal day for constructive activity. Long journeys and travel are highlighted, and you will achieve some degree of personal success. Be careful what you eat.

[**26**] While the day's activities progress peacefully, you will not get through everything you wanted to get done. Any problems in your romantic life are best left unresolved.

[**27**] Prospects for today are good: set about achieving your objectives with confidence. There is a chance of promotion and the prospect of a better financial position. Avoid dark blue.

[**28**] Although there will be minor setbacks today, you will be able to rise above them. There is time for social activity later. Rummage carefully through things you have left untended.

[**29**] This is a particularly demanding, but, nevertheless, highly successful day. Be prepared to put a lot of effort into whatever you do. There are prospects for a rise in social standing.

[**30**] During this stimulating day, you will have the flair to be creative, and may decide to make changes in your personal style. A chance meeting brings benefits later.

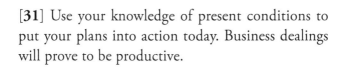

[**31**] Use your knowledge of present conditions to put your plans into action today. Business dealings will prove to be productive.

[**32**] This is a good day for leisure, so take things easily. Although finances are now more secure, try to keep your expenditure to an absolute minimum.

[**33**] Conditions are favourable for all matters to do with your family, social and personal life today. Matters outside the home and family circle are less positive.

[**34**] The day has good aspects, and some less favourable. Rewards come from an unexpected source. There should be moderate success regarding the outcome of personal correspondence.

[**35**] The day brings personal satisfaction for having achieved your goal. At last. But it should not be at the expense of causing friction and jealousy among friends and colleagues.

[**36**] It would be advisable not to get too involved in activities concerning people you have only recently met. Your best achievements will come from the things you do on your own.

[**37**] This is a highly favourable day for the Dragon in all matters concerning the home, whether involving the house and its furnishings, moving, or members of the family. But be careful not to cause offence unwittingly.

[**38**] You should have moderate success today with respect to dealings with land or outdoor matters. There are favourable outcomes for long-term projects which are already well established. Take care of your possessions when travelling.

[**39**] Matters today remain fairly stable. This enables you to get on with the tasks in hand without distractions. You will be offered advice which you should consider carefully.

[**40**] If engaged in dispute, use tact, rather than aggression, to make your point. Carefully check the quality of any prospective purchases. Do not be afraid to change your mind.

[41] While all the signs are for the most part favourable, there may be greater expenditure than was intended. You will impress friends with your decisions.

[42] It is important to take care not to strain your financial resources today. Be prepared for a frustrating time, and keep your head. Avoid unnecessary travel.

[43] All practical matters will be successful today. But heed advice about becoming involved in a relationship with a new acquaintance, whether socially or for business.

[44] Proceed with confidence today in respect of matters to do with career prospects. In other fields, unexpected news will bring great pleasure.

[45] You will have to work hard to make progress today. Antagonism from an unexpected quarter will delay your plans. Keep away from personal confrontation.

[46] The fact that not much is achieved today need not be cause for concern. In dealing with some legal matters, there is only moderate satisfaction.

[47] Today brings great benefits. But expect greater demands to be made of you at work. The more effort you put into your work today, the greater the satisfaction.

[48] This will be a better day for planning than achieving. But more progress can be made if you feel in a creative mood. Use your talents for your own enjoyment.

[49] Matters today remain fairly stable, and it is a good time for friendly discussions. Some physical activity will be beneficial. Make the call you were considering.

[50] For the Dragon personality, this is an ideal time to join in some joint activities with friends or colleagues. The emphasis should be on enjoyment, rather than gain.

[**51**] This will be an enjoyable day, but social events are best when they are with colleagues rather than family. There are also favourable prospects for your career.

[**52**] Do not allow yourself to get irritated by petty setbacks, as this could lead to muddled thinking. There should be success in commercial transactions generally, but today is not a good time for signing documents.

[**53**] There may be some setbacks in your personal life, but matters generally turn out well. The domestic environment is better. Financial improvement is foreseen.

[**54**] It is a good day for dealing with paperwork and legal matters. In tangible, everyday matters, however, conditions are less favourable. Setbacks will only be temporary.

[**55**] Anything to do with career is highlighted for the Dragon today, and it is an opportune time for those seeking promotion. There will be good news regarding family matters.

[56] Ensure that you have ready cash available for an emergency causing you delays. But later the day's events will run smoothly.

[57] The morning will be best for commercial transactions. Later in the day, try to avoid any difficult situations which will demand alert responses, as time will soon run out.

[58] Be careful in your dealings with others today, especially in the late afternoon. Pay attention to the passing of time. There are favourable prospects for family matters.

[59] Conditions begin to change, enabling you to proceed with plans. It will be a very successful day in all respects, particularly if you are thinking of making any alterations to your living arrangements.

[60] [0] This is a most favourable day. Proceed with confidence to achieve your ambitions. Prospects for health, travel, home life, business and romance are all excellent.

About the author

Having written some twenty books over the last 30 years, that have been translated into more than a dozen languages, Derek Walters is an internationally acclaimed authority on traditional Chinese culture.

Derek's original career was in music and in common with many musicians he also had a keen interest in astronomy. This interest led him to study the links and differences between popular Chinese astrology and its western counterpart.

In recognition of his pioneering activities introducing Chinese culture to the west the *International Fengshui Society of Singapore* awarded him the title Honorable Master.

He now lives in the charming seaside town of Morecambe, England, where he once again pursued his musical interests and became the conductor of a men's choir until his retirement in 2020.

Printed in Great Britain
by Amazon

67345901R00054